HERE'S WHAT PEOPLE ARE SAYING ABOUT THIS BOOK:

"This is a valuable book – very concise and clear. It should assist every person in organizing all the important areas of their life."

— **Jarratt G. Bennett,** *CFPtm, ChFC, CLU, Author and Financial Planner*

"This is a remarkable tool to force us to be adults. For anyone who has thrown themselves into their career or moved frequently and not had the time to pay attention to life support details, this guide is a must! I only wish I had had it 20 years ago."

— **Krissa Johnson-Sotomayor,** *Personal Chef and Owner: For The Love Of Cooking, LLC*

"Know Your Life is a simple, yet necessary tool to help manage life's transitions."

— **Catherine Bridgers,** *Business Woman*

"Know Your Life is a practical, well thought-out resource manual to take on life's journey. Every household should own a copy."

— **Henry Jackson,** *Chief Executive Officer, Banneker Capital Management Corporation*

"I am a very organized person, Know Your Life has shown me some new ways to be even more so! It is very encouraging and helpful."

— **Gretchen Ann Morris,** *CISSP, Security Expert*

"I was a family doctor for forty years and have stood at the bedside of hundreds of people as they breathed their last. It saddened me to see how often they had made no preparations and left no directions for the surviving family. If they had used this book, the painful transition would have been one of love and appreciation for the deceased's caring, instead of confusion and helplessness."

— **William H. Orsinger, M.D.** *(retired)*

"Know Your Life is one of the best books to read if you want to prepare for your future. It offers a much needed view into how to get organized, no matter what age or stage of life you are in."

— **Regina Forte,** *co-author of Making the Money Last*

"An excellent job of capturing the essentials and details of planning and preparing for many situations throughout one's life. It provided a tool for me to organize my Mother's affairs in half the time I would have spent just in trying to get organized, and then provided a single resource of information at my fingertips as I worked through every element of her life and her assets."

— **Shirley A. Pierini,** *CPP, President of ASIS International and Vice President Corporate Security and Safety for Ameriquest*

KNOW
Your Life

BY ORGANIZING IT!

James P. Litchko

Tiny Kitchen Publishing
Annandale, VA
www.thetinykitchen.com

KNOW Your Life By Organizing It!
Start managing your life more efficiently and effectively.

By James P. Litchko

Published by:

Tiny Kitchen Publishing
5115 Ravensworth Road
Annandale, VA 22003

thetinykitchen@aol.com
http://www.thetinykitchen.com

Printed in the United States of America
First Edition
Copyright ©2004 James P. Litchko

ISBN 0-9716028-2-4

LCCN 2004105686

This publication is sold with the understanding that the publisher and author is not engaged in rendering legal, accounting, or other professional service. If legal advice or other expert assistance is required, the services of a competent professional should be sought.

Cover and Interior design by: Kristin L. Adolfson

PERSONAL

INCOME

FINANCES

STOCKS

PROPERTY

INSURANCE

MEDICAL

WISHES

Dedicated to my loving mother and father, Maxine and George Litchko, who provided me with the experience to recognize the worth of such a document to help others organize their lives, and my wife Jane who gave me the confidence to write this book.

TABLE OF CONTENTS

INTRODUCTION

How do I organize my life?

Did you ever wish you had the ability to be more effective and efficient when managing and organizing your life? And with that ability, you would save time, gain more control over external demands, and increase your confidence during crisis situations?

That is what *Know Your Life* is about: getting more control of the details that make up your life. If you condense all that information into one location, you're not wasting time looking for items under beds, in shoe boxes, stacks of papers, tattered files, glove compartments, buried tin cans, or even safety deposit boxes. *Know Your Life* provides you with one document to refer to when you need to address your life and financial issues.

We have all lost time and money, or made situations more complicated and frustrating just because we:

- Lost an important document
- Could not find an insurance policy or the deed for a property
- Were unable to validate past employment
- Forgot to renew a subscription or pay a bill
- Did not know a loved one's last wishes

Often this is because your bills, papers and certificates are not organized efficiently. We've all tried vertical files, stacked bins, wire folders, envelopes, stacks of papers, bulletin boards, and lists without success. Many of these methods are not effective because documents vary with different storage and security requirements, and have varying importance at different times of your life.

For example:

- There are different formats for cards, bills, titles, policies, stocks, tax forms, etc.
- Storage and security locations include home files, fire-proof safe, safety deposit box, attorney, accountant, and hospital
- Access frequency is weekly, monthly, semi-annually, annually, post-accident, illness, time-of-death, or random

Know Your Life has been designed to provide you with a procedure and a place to document and/or store all your important papers.

People have found that completing *Know Your Life* has made the effort of doing employment applications, background check submissions, credit and mortgage applications, asset management, passport requests, and retirement planning very efficient. Additionally, the final document provides peace of mind and reduces the confusion, worry and stress related to crisis situations like accidents, divorce, and the death of a loved one.

To *Know Your Life*, you need to assemble all the elements that affect your life: your skills and qualifications, experience, assets, financial and health supports, and your wishes. Specifically in the areas related to your:

- Personal Identity: Birth certificates, passports, driver's licenses
- Income: Employment, retirement, Social Security
- Finances: Bank accounts, credit cards
- Investments: Stocks, bonds
- Properties: House, timeshares, cars, boats
- Insurance: Life, property, car
- Health: Medical plans, hospitals, doctors
- Wishes: Wills, arrangements, notifications

Documenting these categories provides you with a single location and reference when you need this type of information. Whether you need an insurance policy, employment reference, license number, vehicle identification number, lost credit card reference, passport status, or travel history, you can simply go to *Know Your Life* to get the answer. This is the strength of a completed *Know Your Life* book: quick location of key, accurate information.

No matter how young or old you are, it is never too early or late to get one's life under control and increase the efficiency of managing routine and emergency activities. Whether it is for you, a family member, or colleague, *Know Your Life* is a tool that can help you improve the quality of your life.

OVERALL GUIDANCE TO KNOW YOUR LIFE

This book was created to be a living document: a template, tool, and reference of the key elements of your life. It is meant to support you and others during a crisis and in routine times. From paying bills to covering all your bases, this book is meant to be a simple guide for organizing your life for yourself and others.

FORMAT: *Know Your Life* consists of fill-in-the-blank and add-references-as-desired areas to provide customization and flexibility for most individuals.

Fill-in-the-blank spaces are for entering names, addresses, document numbers, phone numbers, names of companies, agencies, etc. These are provided to help you with identifying the pertinent information you may need. They are not provided as a checklist for things that you must do, like buy stocks, get a broker or lawyer, or buy insurance.

Additionally, you should never feel obligated to fill in what you think would be very sensitive information. An alternate option would be to indicate in the book that "the information can be found in…"

The workbook format suggests adding-references-as-desired, including actual or copies of important documents you need. Including documents in the workbook gives you a physical location for these papers and makes it easy to update the book on a monthly, quarterly, or annual basis.

GROWTH: *Know Your Life* is designed to provide you with the most options. The book lays flat when open to make reviews and updates easier. It is standard letter size to easily fit in a desk drawer or fireproof box, and large enough to hold most documents. The soft-cover allows the book to be folded length-wise for storing in a safety deposit box or small home safe.

The perforated heavier paper supports those that prefer to remove the pages and transfer the book to a ringed binder. Past users have added tab dividers, with or without pockets, to facilitate document inclusion. If you prefer to use dividers, you can download instructions and guidelines at http://www.knowyourlife.com.

APPROACH: There are several ways you can complete this book. You can tackle the entire thing at once, or one section at a time. It is recommended, however, to go from beginning to end, as *Know Your Life* was designed in a specific order to increase efficiency and reduce frustration.

No matter which approach you use, do one page at a time and keep a list or mark those items where you need to go back and add more information, or where you need to include copies of important documents. This will allow you to move aggressively along and to gain confidence in managing your life.

DETAILS: Remember that making a note like "the title of the car is held by the First National Bank until the car loan is paid" is an acceptable way to indicate where certain documents are located, and will be very helpful to those select individuals who may need to access them if you are unable.

UPDATING: Because *Know Your Life* is a living document, you will need to occasionally update the information. It is convenient to do this on a quarterly or semi-annual basis. As you receive new changes, financial documents, policies, properties, valuables, etc., place the new document or copy in the related section of the book and put it aside. Then periodically pull the book out and update the entire document at one time.

AWARENESS: One of the keys to maintaining a strong relationship is the sharing of information with one's partner, guardian, or caregiver. This book facilitates the sharing of financial and personal information and setting goals with others in an organized and informal way. One of the best times to do this is after one of the periodic updates.

TICKLER: Transform *Know Your Life* into a tickler system. Sticky notes or other small pieces of paper can be marked with the date when something is due and placed at the top of the corresponding page. This can be done for all recurring actions like annual visits to doctors, semi-annual visits to dentists, paying taxes, updating valuable items for personal property insurance, annual changing of batteries in fire alarms, or knowing when your employment evaluation is due.

SENSITIVITY WARNING: Most importantly, remember while you are completing this book you will be creating a sensitive record that provides personal details of your life. This document should be protected in a manner that you think is appropriate, or sensitive items should be separately secured in a safe location identified only to trusted individuals.

CAUTIONS: This document does not provide professional, financial, or legal advice. When you are making financial and/or legal decisions, seek guidance from professionals in those areas. Additionally, although there is a section in this book where you indicate your wishes for certain possessions after you die, this is not a legally binding will. In order to make these desires formal and legal, be sure to document your wishes in your actual will.

SUGGESTIONS: As you document your life, you may find more items you would like to add that are not identified in the book, or you may come up with recommendations that could help others to know their life.

Please send these to suggestions@knowyourlife.com, with your name and contact information and we will include these in future updates so that others may benefit from them.

REFERENCES: To further support your efforts in knowing your life, periodically check the website http://www.knowyourlife.com for suggestions and helpful hints from others and additional references.

APPRECIATION

There are so many that I want to thank, my gratitude especially goes to friends, family and those from the hospice organization that supported my mother before, during and after the death of my father. At this critical time, she exhibited amazing organization and confidence as a result of using *Know Your Life*.

Secondly, I want to thank my friends from different religions, ethnic backgrounds, and ages that reviewed and provided recommendations to improve this book. These include: Regina Forte, Noelle Hardy, Dr. Adrienne Jackson, Paul Byron Pattak, Shirley Pierini, CPP, Karen and Bob Safer, Shirley and Ed Schussel, Kara Graham, Gayle Reuter, Catherine Bridgers, Gretchen Ann Morris, and my editor, Kristin Adolfson.

Finally, my loving thanks to my mother and to my wife, both of whom provided the confidence, encouragement, and incentive for making this document something that can be used by many to know their life.

KNOW

You are on the road to
organizing your life!

PERSONAL

PERSONAL

PERSONAL

Who am I and how do I prove it to others?

Knowing your life begins with documenting your identity as established in your personal documents. These papers document your name, who you are or who you were, where you're from and where you can go. Many of these documents verify citizenship, age, and origin, which are necessary to obtain additional documents and authorizations such as passports or security clearances.

The information and documents in this section are very sensitive and you need to make sure that they are strongly protected. These are the key documents that prove your identity, and they are also the key documents someone needs to steal your identity. In the unfortunate circumstance that you are the victim of identity theft, you may need this information to prove your identity.

Identity theft is a fast growing crime in our society. It is not only when someone steals your credit card number and uses it to make purchases, but also when they use your name, birthday, Social Security number and any other personal information to establish new loans, credit cards, mortgages and other things under your identity. This is a very serious crime that can have a major impact on your life, so it is highly recommended that you secure this book, contents, as well as any original documents in a very safe place.

Ensure that you carefully document each entry accurately and clearly. Be especially careful that you record your name exactly as it is printed on the document listed.

Record the location of each key document, include a reference number, as in a license or certificate number, date, and originating organization, like a city or state government, church or firm. All of this information will help you if the document is lost and you need to prove its existence.

In *Personal*, document any jobs you've held and contact information for people that you could use as personal and professional references. This information is important when filling out resumes or job applications, and can also be required when looking for employment or residence in another country.

Your current and past residential addresses and travel history are important if you are considering a job where you could be working with sensitive or classified information and would need to have a background check, such as a bank, intelligence agency, casino, or jewelry store. When applying, this information will allow you to quickly fill out the appropriate forms.

Finally, it is a good idea to include paper and/or electronic copies of various resumes and background applications in this section. An alternative would be to make a notation as to where they can be found if they are in an alternate location.

KNOW YOUR LIFE - ORGANIZE YOUR PERSONAL DOCUMENTS!

PERSONAL

KNOW

With every entry, this document further describes your identity. Protect this workbook to that level of sensitivity.

NAME DOCUMENTS:

Listed here are the documents that formally verify your name. This list can include birth certificates, passports, drivers' license, military identification, social security, immigration papers, baptismal records, name change documents, adoption papers, and citizenship papers.

Type of Document: _____

Name: _____   Reference Number: _____
     (exact name as on document)

Originating Organization: _____

Address: _____

_____

Location of Document: _____

Type of Document: _____

Name: _____   Reference Number: _____
     (exact name as on document)

Originating Organization: _____

Address: _____

_____

Location of Document: _____

Type of Document: _____

Name: _____   Reference Number: _____
     (exact name as on document)

Originating Organization: _____

Address: _____

_____

Location of Document: _____

NAME DOCUMENTS continued

Type of Document: _____

Name: _____ Reference Number: _____
(exact name as on document)

Originating Organization: _____

Address: _____

_____

Location of Document: _____

Type of Document: _____

Name: _____ Reference Number: _____
(exact name as on document)

Originating Organization: _____

Address: _____

_____

Location of Document: _____

Type of Document: _____

Name: _____ Reference Number: _____
(exact name as on document)

Originating Organization: _____

Address: _____

_____

Location of Document: _____

NAME DOCUMENTS continued

Type of Document: _____

Name: _____ Reference Number: _____
(exact name as on document)

Originating Organization: _____

Address: _____

_____

Location of Document: _____

Type of Document: _____

Name: _____ Reference Number: _____
(exact name as on document)

Originating Organization: _____

Address: _____

_____

Location of Document: _____

Type of Document: _____

Name: _____ Reference Number: _____
(exact name as on document)

Originating Organization: _____

Address: _____

_____

Location of Document: _____

PERSONAL

PARTNERSHIP DOCUMENTS:

Marriage licenses, prenuptial agreements, and divorce papers are examples of various partnership documents you may have.

Type of Document: _____

Reference Number: _____

Originating Organization: _____

Address: _____

_____

Location of Document: _____

Type of Document: _____

Reference Number: _____

Originating Organization: _____

Address: _____

_____

Location of Document: _____

Type of Document: _____

Reference Number: _____

Originating Organization: _____

Address: _____

_____

Location of Document: _____

PARTNERSHIP DOCUMENTS continued

Type of Document: _____

Reference Number: _____

Originating Organization: _____

Address: _____

_____

Location of Document: _____

Type of Document: _____

Reference Number: _____

Originating Organization: _____

Address: _____

_____

Location of Document: _____

Type of Document: _____

Reference Number: _____

Originating Organization: _____

Address: _____

_____

Location of Document: _____

PERSONAL

KNOW

Making copies of both sides of licenses, medical, and financial cards can be very helpful if they need to be replaced or renewed.

EDUCATION:

Maintaining a record of schooling and training is helpful when applying for jobs, volunteer positions, other schools, etc. Your educational experience is also necessary to qualify for professional certifications (documented in the next section). Consider starting with high school and include any trade school, college, or special skills training. If you have made a favorable impression on your teachers, advisors, or other persons, ask them if they would be a reference for you in the future, and record them in this section.

Institution: _____ Date(s): _____

Address: _____

_____

Phone: _____ Website: _____

Your Name: _____
(exact name as on document)

References (Names and Contact Information): _____

_____

_____

Location of Letters of Reference: _____

Institution: _____ Date(s): _____

Address: _____

_____

Phone: _____ Website: _____

Your Name: _____
(exact name as on document)

References (Names and Contact Information): _____

_____

_____

Location of Letters of Reference: _____

_____

EDUCATION continued

Institution: _____ Date(s): _____

Address: _____

_____

Phone: _____ Website: _____

Your Name: _____
(exact name as on document)

References (Names and Contact Information): _____

_____

_____

Location of Letters of Reference: _____

Institution: _____ Date(s): _____

Address: _____

_____

Phone: _____ Website: _____

Your Name: _____
(exact name as on document)

References (Names and Contact Information): _____

_____

_____

Location of Letters of Reference: _____

EDUCATION continued

Institution: _____ Date(s): _____

Address: _____

_____

Phone: _____ Website: _____

Your Name: _____
(exact name as on document)

References (Names and Contact Information): _____

_____

_____

Location of Letters of Reference: _____

Institution: _____ Date(s): _____

Address: _____

_____

Phone: _____ Website: _____

Your Name: _____
(exact name as on document)

References (Names and Contact Information): _____

_____

_____

Location of Letters of Reference: _____

KNOW

Make sure to record the spelling of your name and all reference numbers exactly as they appear on the document.

PROFESSIONAL CERTIFICATIONS:

There are several documents that certify your professional credentials. These include but are not limited to: high school or college diplomas, teacher credentials, or certifications such as CPA, M.D., CISSP, CPP, Certified Massage Expert, Certified Palm Reader, Licensed Nurse, Certified Scuba Diver Certificate, Pilot's License, Licensed Welder, Radio Operator's License, and Chauffeur's Licenses, to name a few.

Type of Document: _____

Your Name: _____ Reference Number: _____
(exact name as on document)

Originating Organization: _____

Address: _____

_____

Location of Document: _____ Date Acquired: _____

Type of Document: _____

Your Name: _____ Reference Number: _____
(exact name as on document)

Originating Organization: _____

Address: _____

_____

Location of Document: _____ Date Acquired: _____

PERSONAL

PROFESSIONAL CERTIFICATIONS continued

Type of Document: _____

Your Name: _____ Reference Number: _____
(exact name as on document)

Originating Organization: _____

Address: _____

_____

Location of Document: _____ Date Acquired: _____

Type of Document: _____

Your Name: _____ Reference Number: _____
(exact name as on document)

Originating Organization: _____

Address: _____

_____

Location of Document: _____ Date Acquired: _____

Type of Document: _____

Your Name: _____ Reference Number: _____
(exact name as on document)

Originating Organization: _____

Address: _____

_____

Location of Document: _____ Date Acquired: _____

WORK HISTORY AND REFERENCES:

It is useful to keep a record of where you've worked or volunteered. This type of record can help when developing a resume or completing a job application. Just like in your educational experiences, you will demonstrate for others what kind of worker you are, so it is good to document additional references like bosses, community representatives, social workers, volunteer coordinators, rabbis, priests, ministers, or other persons with whom you have had any kind of professional relationship.

Organization: _____

Title: _____ Date(s): _____

Address: _____

_____

Phone Number: _____ Website: _____

Your Name: _____
              (exact name as on document)

References (Names and Contact Information): _____

_____

_____

Location of Letter of Reference: _____

PERSONAL

WORK HISTORY AND REFERENCES continued

Organization: _____

Title: _____ Date(s): _____

Address: _____

_____

Phone Number: _____ Website: _____

Your Name: _____
             (exact name as on document)

References (Names and Contact Information): _____

_____

_____

Location of Letter of Reference: _____

Organization: _____

Title: _____ Date(s): _____

Address: _____

_____

Phone Number: _____ Website: _____

Your Name: _____
             (exact name as on document)

References (Names and Contact Information): _____

_____

_____

Location of Letter of Reference: _____

WORK HISTORY AND REFERENCES continued

Organization: _____

Title: _____ Date(s): _____

Address: _____

_____

Phone Number: _____ Website: _____

Your Name: _____
(exact name as on document)

References (Names and Contact Information): _____

_____

_____

Location of Letter of Reference: _____

Organization: _____

Title: _____ Date(s): _____

Address: _____

_____

Phone Number: _____ Website: _____

Your Name: _____
(exact name as on document)

References (Names and Contact Information): _____

_____

_____

Location of Letter of Reference: _____

PERSONAL

ADDRESS HISTORY:

In some cases certain financial, security, military, and intelligence related employers will ask you to provide a history of where you've lived and traveled outside of the country, therefore it is a good idea to keep track of any change of address and overseas travel.

Be sure to identify the dates that you lived at the location and if the residence was a private home, condominium, apartment, or organization.

Dates   Type of Residence   Address

_____

_____

_____

_____

_____

_____

_____

_____

_____

_____

_____

_____

_____

_____

_____

TRAVEL HISTORY:

Frequently, background applications ask for the name of a person, organization, or document that can verify the location and reason of travel (i.e., pleasure or business). They normally do not ask for the address of the residence or hotel where you stayed, so it is only necessary to list the the city and country where the travel took place.

Dates	Reason	City and Country	Verifier

PERSONAL

TRAVEL HISTORY continued

Dates   Reason   City and Country   Verifier

_____

_____

_____

_____

_____

_____

_____

_____

_____

_____

_____

_____

_____

_____

_____

_____

_____

_____

_____

TRAVEL HISTORY continued

Dates   Reason   City and Country   Verifier

PERSONAL

ACTIONS/NOTES:

PERSONAL

INCOME

INCOME

INCOME

Where do you get your income?

Income information is often easy to obtain. Begin with getting copies of your last income tax, pay and bank statements. These documents will provide a good start on identifying your various sources of income and retirement accounts. Consider attaching a copy of these annual statements in this book for reference.

When you have your income information organized, it is not just beneficial for tax purposes. You will need income information when you apply for a loan, document your job references, build your resume, complete applications of background checks, and so on.

Just like in the previous section, ensure that you record your name and related identification numbers exactly as listed by the employer or institution at the time of employment. Accuracy will make audits and validation of employment much more efficient.

Remember that name changes, use of nicknames, or aliases can provide major problems when you or others are trying to verify past information for future employment purposes or long term employment benefits. These need to be documented as well.

In the *Personal* section you documented your past work history. As you start to fill out the Pay and Retirement portions of this section, you may feel that you are duplicating your input. Many have found that the duplication makes using the document more effective. If you do not want duplicate entries, put a note that refers to the previous page where you have already input the information.

If you are using this book to support your tickler system, *Income* is where you would identify when annual or semi-annual evaluations are due, when you are eligible for social security benefits, the date you can retire, etc.

KNOW YOUR LIFE - ORGANIZE YOUR INCOME!

INCOME

KNOW

Know Your Life can serve as a great tickler system. See the Introduction, page XIV.

INCOME TAX

It is recommended that you enclose a copy of the last two years of federal, state and local income tax returns, as appropriate.

Location of copies of past income tax submissions and those of the people you are responsible for:

_____

_____

_____

_____

Persons or firms that assisted you with preparing your taxes:

_____

_____

_____

_____

Notes on income tax statements:

_____

_____

_____

_____

INCOME

INCOME

PAY

Government, military, and corporate organizations use different terms for income documentation, therefore there are three seperate sections under Pay. You need only to complete the section which applies to your employment.

Some organizations use Employee Identification Numbers (EIN) to track their employees and others use the individual's Social Security Number (SSN). The military used to use Military Identification Numbers until they switched to using the individual's SSN. Complete this line with whichever identification number is or was used by your employer. The actual name that you used during employment is also very important for tracking purposes, so each employment area asks for the exact name that accounting and human resources used in formal documents at that company.

You may also want to enclose a copy of your annual pay summary in the form of a W-2, 1099, etc.

CORPORATE

Company Name: _____

Employee Name: _____
(exact name as on employment contract or paycheck)

EIN/SSN: _____

Position: _____

Dates of Employment: _____

Headquarters Office Location: _____ Phone: _____

Address: _____

_____

Web Site Address: _____

Location of Pay Statements: _____

CORPORATE continued

Company Name: _____

Employee Name: _____
(exact name as on employment contract or paycheck)

EIN/SSN: _____

Position: _____

Dates of Employment: _____

Headquarters Office Location: _____ Phone: _____

Address: _____

_____

Web Site Address: _____

Location of Pay Statements: _____

Company Name: _____

Employee Name: _____
(exact name as on employment contract or paycheck)

EIN/SSN: _____

Position: _____

Dates of Employment: _____

Headquarters Office Location: _____ Phone: _____

Address: _____

_____

Web Site Address: _____

Location of Pay Statements: _____

INCOME

KNOW

Input your name exactly as it is recorded on organizational documents so file searches can be more effective and efficient.

GOVERNMENT

Service or Agency Name: _____

Employee Name: _____
(exact name as on employment contract or paycheck)

EIN/SSN: _____

Title: _____

Dates of Service: _____

Headquarters Office Location: _____ Phone: _____

Address: _____

_____

Web Site Address: _____

Location of Pay Statements: _____

INCOME

Service or Agency Name: _____

Employee Name: _____
(exact name as on employment contract or paycheck)

EIN/SSN: _____

Title: _____

Dates of Service: _____

Headquarters Office Location: _____ Phone: _____

Address: _____

_____

Web Site Address: _____

Location of Pay Statements: _____

INCOME

MILITARY

It is recommended that you enclose a copy of your discharge papers (Form DD-214) and an annual pay summary.

Service: _____

Employee Name: _____
(exact name as on employment contract or paycheck)

Military Identification Number: _____

Rank/Rate: _____ Dates of Service: _____

Veteran's Affairs Office Location: _____ Phone: _____

Address: _____

_____

Web Site Address: _____

Type of Discharge: _____

Location of Pay Statements: _____

Service: _____

Employee Name: _____
(exact name as on employment contract or paycheck)

Military Identification Number: _____

Rank/Rate: _____ Dates of Service: _____

Veteran's Affairs Office Location: _____ Phone: _____

Address: _____

_____

Web Site Address: _____

Type of Discharge: _____

Location of Pay Statements: _____

INCOME

SOCIAL SECURITY

The Social Security Administration annually sends out a statement of your benefits and what you can expect to receive when you are eligible for these benefits. Attach that document in this section. Additional information about your Social Security benefits can be found on their website: http://www.ssa.gov

Full Name   Social Security Number

_____   _____

_____   _____

For reference purposes it is helpful to list the SSNs for other individuals in your family, such as spouses, parents, and children. Because of the sensitivity of this information, be sure to ask the individuals for permission to document their information here:

Full Name   Relationship   Social Security Number

_____   _____   _____

_____   _____   _____

_____   _____   _____

_____   _____   _____

_____   _____   _____

_____   _____   _____

_____   _____   _____

_____   _____   _____

_____   _____   _____

INCOME

KNOW

Reduce the sensitivity of this book. Consider placing your confidential documents in an alternative location, safety deposit box or vault, and identify that location in this book.

RETIREMENT

Retirement plans vary widely. Plans specific to the corporate sector are the Defined Contribution Plan 401(k), Defined Benefit Plan (many old companies had these types of pension plans), and Employee Stock Option Plan (ESOP). The government sector has the Thrift Savings Plan (TSP), and the military has the Military Pension Plan.

Many of these plans have surviving spouse options where, if the employee dies, the surviving spouse will continue to receive a percentage of the payments for the rest of their life.

When inquiring into a deceased employee's retirement plans, be sure to ask the company about the deceased's participation in corporate profit sharing plans, vested stock options, bonuses, additional wages due to the employee, vacation and sick leave reimbursements, and any disability payments.

Be sure to enclose a copy of any annual statements for your retirement plans.

RETIREMENT PLANS:

Name of Plan: _____

Type of Plan: _____

Employee Name: _____ EIN/SSN: _____
(exact name as on plan)

Company of Employment: _____

Plan Headquarters Office: _____ Phone: _____

Address: _____

_____

Web Site Address: _____

Location of Pay Statements: _____

Surviving Spouse: _____

Surviving Spouse Terms: _____

INCOME

RETIREMENT continued

Name of Plan: _____

Type of Plan: _____

Employee Name: _____ EIN/SSN: _____
(exact name as on plan)

Company of Employment: _____

Plan Headquarters Office: _____ Phone: _____

Address: _____

_____

Web Site Address: _____

Location of Pay Statements: _____

Surviving Spouse: _____

Surviving Spouse Terms: _____

Name of Plan: _____

Type of Plan: _____

Employee Name: _____ EIN/SSN: _____
(exact name as on plan)

Company of Employment: _____

Plan Headquarters Office: _____ Phone: _____

Address: _____

_____

Web Site Address: _____

Location of Pay Statements: _____

Surviving Spouse: _____

Surviving Spouse Terms: _____

RETIREMENT continued

Name of Plan: _____

Type of Plan: _____

Employee Name: _____ EIN/SSN: _____
(exact name as on plan)

Company of Employment: _____

Plan Headquarters Office: _____ Phone: _____

Address: _____

_____

Web Site Address: _____

Location of Pay Statements: _____

Surviving Spouse: _____

Surviving Spouse Terms: _____

Name of Plan: _____

Type of Plan: _____

Employee Name: _____ EIN/SSN: _____
(exact name as on plan)

Company of Employment: _____

Plan Headquarters Office: _____ Phone: _____

Address: _____

_____

Web Site Address: _____

Location of Pay Statements: _____

Surviving Spouse: _____

Surviving Spouse Terms: _____

INCOME

401(K)s

Company: _____

Owner's Name: _____
(exact name as on plan)

Account Number: _____

Custodial Company: _____

Address: _____ Investor Service Phone: _____

_____

Location of Statements: _____

Beneficiary: _____

Company: _____

Owner's Name: _____
(exact name as on plan)

Account Number: _____

Custodial Company: _____

Address: _____ Investor Service Phone: _____

_____

Location of Statements: _____

Beneficiary: _____

IRAs

Financial Institution: _____

Owner's Name: _____
(exact name as on plan)

Account Number: _____

Broker/Agent's Name: _____ Phone: _____

Address: _____

_____

Location of Statements: _____

Beneficiary: _____

Financial Institution: _____

Owner's Name: _____
(exact name as on plan)

Account Number: _____

Broker/Agent's Name: _____ Phone: _____

Address: _____

_____

Location of Statements: _____

Beneficiary: _____

INCOME

INCOME

IRAs continued

Financial Institution: _____

Owner's Name: _____
(exact name as on plan)

Account Number: _____

Broker/Agent's Name: _____ Phone: _____

Address: _____

_____

Location of Statements: _____

Beneficiary: _____

Financial Institution: _____

Owner's Name: _____
(exact name as on plan)

Account Number: _____

Broker/Agent's Name: _____ Phone: _____

Address: _____

_____

Location of Statements: _____

Beneficiary: _____

RETIREMENT ASSOCIATIONS

Association: _____

Member's Name: _____
(exact name as on member's association membership card)

Membership Number: _____

Chapter: _____

Local Point of Contact: _____ Phone: _____

Headquarters Phone: _____

Address: _____

_____

Web Site Address: _____

Association: _____

Member's Name: _____
(exact name as on member's association membership card)

Membership Number: _____

Chapter: _____

Local Point of Contact: _____ Phone: _____

Headquarters Phone: _____

Address: _____

_____

Web Site Address: _____

INCOME

KNOW

Congratulations! You are on your way to completing this book.

ACTIONS/NOTES:

INCOME

FINANCES

FINANCES

FINANCES

Where is your money?

Finances identifies areas where funds are available for use if needed for immediate and future expenses. These areas include: savings and checking accounts, money market accounts, credit cards, and certificates of deposit (CDs). Additionally, this section identifies where funds are owed, such as loans for property and past services, like educational loans.

The final part of *Finances* refers to the owners' responsibilities for the finances of others. When trusts or eldercare are taken on by another individual, the financial arrangement should be documented, so that there is never a loss of continuity in support to those individuals.

To complete *Finances*, start gathering the annual summaries and/or monthly or quarterly statements from loan companies, accounting firms, banks, and so on. Attach copies of these statements to this section for quick reference.

In support of a tickler system, you can identify when renewals are due, such as credit cards, CDs, etc.

FINANCES

KNOW YOUR LIFE - ORGANIZE YOUR FINANCES!

KNOW

This book was developed to organize your life, not as a checklist of what you have to do in life.

ACCOUNTANTS AND ADVISORS

Accounting Firm: _____

Name: _____ Phone: _____

Address: _____

_____

Tax Preparer: _____

Name: _____ Phone: _____

Address: _____

_____

Financial Advisor's Firm: _____

Name: _____ Phone: _____

Address: _____

_____

Banker: _____

Name: _____ Phone: _____

Address: _____

_____

Attorney: _____

Name: _____ Phone: _____

Address: _____

_____

FINANCES

FINANCES

SAVINGS, CHECKING AND MONEY MARKET ACCOUNTS

Financial Institution: _____

Account Number: _____

Owner's Name(s): _____
(exact name as on account)

Representative's Name: _____ Phone: _____

Address: _____

_____

Location of Books/Statements: _____

Financial Institution: _____

Account Number: _____

Owner's Name(s): _____
(exact name as on account)

Representative's Name: _____ Phone: _____

Address: _____

_____

Location of Books/Statements: _____

Financial Institution: _____

Account Number: _____

Owner's Name(s): _____
(exact name as on account)

Representative's Name: _____ Phone: _____

Address: _____

_____

Location of Books/Statements: _____

SAVINGS, CHECKING AND MONEY MARKET ACCOUNTS continued

Financial Institution: _____

Account Number: _____

Owner's Name(s): _____
(exact name as on account)

Representative's Name: _____ Phone: _____

Address: _____

_____

Location of Books/Statements: _____

Financial Institution: _____

Account Number: _____

Owner's Name(s): _____
(exact name as on account)

Representative's Name: _____ Phone: _____

Address: _____

_____

Location of Books/Statements: _____

Financial Institution: _____

Account Number: _____

Owner's Name(s): _____
(exact name as on account)

Representative's Name: _____ Phone: _____

Address: _____

_____

Location of Books/Statements: _____

FINANCES

FINANCES

KNOW

Enter the information clearly, because this book may be used by others to organize the end of your life.

CERTIFICATES OF DEPOSIT (CDs)

CD Institution	Serial Number	Owner's Name(s) (exact name as on certificate)	Amount/Due Date	Location

FINANCES

CDs continued

CD Institution	Serial Number	Owner's Name(s) (exact name as on certificate)	Amount/Due Date	Location

FINANCES

CDs continued

CD Institution	Serial Number	Owner's Name(s) (exact name as on certificate)	Amount/Due Date	Location

_____

SAVINGS BONDS

Savings Bond Type (EE, H, etc.)	Serial Number	Owner's Name(s) (exact name as on bond)	Amount/Due Date	Location

FINANCES

_____

_____

_____

_____

_____

_____

_____

_____

SAVINGS BONDS continued

Savings Bond Type
(EE, H, etc.)

Serial Number

Owner's Name(s)
(exact name as on bond)

Amount/Due Date

Location

FINANCES

OTHER TYPE OF CERTIFICATE

Type of Certificate	Serial Number	Owner's Name(s) (exact name as on certificate)	Amount/Due Date	Location

OTHER TYPE OF CERTIFICATE continued

Type of Certificate	Serial Number	Owner's Name(s) (exact name as on certificate)	Amount/Due Date	Location

KNOW

It is a good idea for your own security to record or store keys, passwords, PIN numbers, and safe combinations in a location other than this book.

CREDIT CARDS AND ATM CARDS

Credit cards, ATM, and debit cards are used extensively in our society. It is important to have a record of these for two reasons: loss and impact on credit record. If your cards are stolen or lost, you will have the information necessary to report the cards' status.

It is recommended that at least once a year you make a copy of all the cards in your purse or wallet, so that you have a copy of the exact card for your records. Additionally, consider attaching a copy of one of your monthly statements in this section for reference.

Card: _____ Type: _____ Institution: _____

Owner's Name(s): _____
(exact name as on card)

Card Number: _____ Expiration Date: _____

Financial Organization: _____ Phone: _____

Address: _____

_____

Location of Card/Statements: _____

Card: _____ Type: _____ Institution: _____

Owner's Name(s): _____
(exact name as on card)

Card Number: _____ Expiration Date: _____

Financial Organization: _____ Phone: _____

Address: _____

_____

Location of Card/Statements: _____

FINANCES

CREDIT CARDS AND ATM CARDS continued

Card: _____ Type: _____ Institution: _____

Owner's Name(s): _____
(exact name as on card)

Card Number: _____ Expiration Date: _____

Financial Organization: _____ Phone: _____

Address: _____

_____

Location of Card/Statements: _____

Card: _____ Type: _____ Institution: _____

Owner's Name(s): _____
(exact name as on card)

Card Number: _____ Expiration Date: _____

Financial Organization: _____ Phone: _____

Address: _____

_____

Location of Card/Statements: _____

Card: _____ Type: _____ Institution: _____

Owner's Name(s): _____
(exact name as on card)

Card Number: _____ Expiration Date: _____

Financial Organization: _____ Phone: _____

Address: _____

_____

Location of Card/Statements: _____

CREDIT CARDS AND ATM CARDS continued

Card: _____ Type: _____ Institution: _____

Owner's Name(s): _____

(exact name as on card)

Card Number: _____ Expiration Date: _____

Financial Organization: _____ Phone: _____

Address: _____

_____

Location of Card/Statements: _____

Card: _____ Type: _____ Institution: _____

Owner's Name(s): _____

(exact name as on card)

Card Number: _____ Expiration Date: _____

Financial Organization: _____ Phone: _____

Address: _____

_____

Location of Card/Statements: _____

Card: _____ Type: _____ Institution: _____

Owner's Name(s): _____

(exact name as on card)

Card Number: _____ Expiration Date: _____

Financial Organization: _____ Phone: _____

Address: _____

_____

Location of Card/Statements: _____

FINANCES

LOANS

List any home, car, business, college, luxury item, or other loans you are currently making payments on.

Financial Institution: _____ Loan Number: _____

Owner's Name(s): _____
(exact name as on account)

Representative's Name: _____ Phone: _____

Address: _____

_____

Location of Books/Statements: _____

Related Insurance Policy: _____

Financial Institution: _____ Loan Number: _____

Owner's Name(s): _____
(exact name as on account)

Representative's Name: _____ Phone: _____

Address: _____

_____

Location of Books/Statements: _____

Related Insurance Policy: _____

LOANS continued

Financial Institution: _____ Loan Number: _____

Owner's Name(s): _____
(exact name as on account)

Representative's Name: _____ Phone: _____

Address: _____

_____

Location of Books/Statements: _____

Related Insurance Policy: _____

Financial Institution: _____ Loan Number: _____

Owner's Name(s): _____
(exact name as on account)

Representative's Name: _____ Phone: _____

Address: _____

_____

Location of Books/Statements: _____

Related Insurance Policy: _____

Financial Institution: _____ Loan Number: _____

Owner's Name(s): _____
(exact name as on account)

Representative's Name: _____ Phone: _____

Address: _____

_____

Location of Books/Statements: _____

Related Insurance Policy: _____

FINANCES

LOANS continued

Financial Institution: _____ Loan Number: _____

Owner's Name(s): _____
(exact name as on account)

Representative's Name: _____ Phone: _____

Address: _____

_____

Location of Books/Statements: _____

Related Insurance Policy: _____

Financial Institution: _____ Loan Number: _____

Owner's Name(s): _____
(exact name as on account)

Representative's Name: _____ Phone: _____

Address: _____

_____

Location of Books/Statements: _____

Related Insurance Policy: _____

Financial Institution: _____ Loan Number: _____

Owner's Name(s): _____
(exact name as on account)

Representative's Name: _____ Phone: _____

Address: _____

_____

Location of Books/Statements: _____

Related Insurance Policy: _____

LOANS continued

Financial Institution: _____ Loan Number: _____

Owner's Name(s): _____
(exact name as on account)

Representative's Name: _____ Phone: _____

Address: _____

_____

Location of Books/Statements: _____

Related Insurance Policy: _____

Financial Institution: _____ Loan Number: _____

Owner's Name(s): _____
(exact name as on account)

Representative's Name: _____ Phone: _____

Address: _____

_____

Location of Books/Statements: _____

Related Insurance Policy: _____

Financial Institution: _____ Loan Number: _____

Owner's Name(s): _____
(exact name as on account)

Representative's Name: _____ Phone: _____

Address: _____

_____

Location of Books/Statements: _____

Related Insurance Policy: _____

FINANCES

KNOW

Think twice and then once again before sharing this book with others. Personal information can be dangerous and hurtful if used maliciously.

RESPONSIBILITIES TO OTHERS:

Document your responsibilities to other individuals such as financial and/or healthcare for a younger or older person in this section. Record the various relationships with the individuals and related professionals, such as doctors, lawyers, or financial institutions, and identify the relevant documents, powers of attorney, contracts, or financial documents. Each situation is different, so this section is flexible to document your individual responsibility.

Name: _____ Phone: _____

Address: _____

_____

Responsibility: _____

Background: _____

_____

_____

_____

_____

Name: _____ Phone: _____

Address: _____

_____

Responsibility: _____

Background: _____

_____

_____

_____

_____

FINANCES

FINANCES

RESPONSIBILITIES TO OTHERS continued

Name: _____ Phone: _____

Address: _____

_____

Responsibility: _____

Background: _____

_____

_____

_____

_____

Name: _____ Phone: _____

Address: _____

_____

Responsibility: _____

Background: _____

_____

_____

_____

_____

RESPONSIBILITIES TO OTHERS continued

Name: _____ Phone: _____

Address: _____

_____

Responsibility: _____

Background: _____

_____

_____

_____

_____

Name: _____ Phone: _____

Address: _____

_____

Responsibility: _____

Background: _____

_____

_____

_____

_____

FINANCES

FINANCES

ACTIONS/NOTES:

FINANCES

STOCKS

STOCKS

STOCKS

Where do you keep your stock certificates?

In *Stocks* you document your stock portfolio. While filling out this section be sure that you include any corporate stocks you hold, any government or corporate bonds that you have, and identify where the certificates are located.

When identifying stocks that are held by brokers, you can include one of the monthly or quarterly summary reports provided by the brokers. For stocks, bonds, and mutual funds whose certificates you personally hold, list each certificate with serial numbers and storage locations.

In those situations where company stock options are available to you, list the stock and include a copy of the employment agreement that spells out the amount and price of the shares, plus vesting and purchase terms.

It is also important that you identify the purchase price and date, because this has an impact on how much you will have to pay in capital gains tax.

STOCKS

KNOW YOUR LIFE - ORGANIZE YOUR STOCKS!

STOCKS

KNOW

It is a good idea to update and review *Know Your Life* once a year.

STOCK BROKERS

Financial Institution: _____ Account Number: _____

Owner's Name(s): _____
(exact name as on account)

Representative's Name: _____ Phone: _____

Address: _____

_____

Location of Statements: _____

Financial Institution: _____ Account Number: _____

Owner's Name(s): _____
(exact name as on account)

Representative's Name: _____ Phone: _____

Address: _____

_____

Location of Statements: _____

Financial Institution: _____ Account Number: _____

Owner's Name(s): _____
(exact name as on account)

Representative's Name: _____ Phone: _____

Address: _____

_____

Location of Statements: _____

KNOW

Brokers often hold the stock certificates. Indicate if that is the case in your situation.

LIST OF STOCKS

Stock Symbol	Number of Shares	Purchase Date	Purchase Price	Owner's Name(s) (exact name as on certificate)	Location

STOCKS

STOCKS continued

Stock Symbol	Number of Shares	Purchase Date	Purchase Price	Owner's Name(s) (exact name as on certificate)	Location

STOCKS

STOCKS continued

Stock Symbol	Number of Shares	Purchase Date	Purchase Price	Owner's Name(s) (exact name as on certificate)	Location

STOCKS

STOCKS

LIST OF MUTUAL FUNDS

Organization Name	Account Number	Number of Shares	Owner's Name(s) (exact name as on certificate)	Location

MUTUAL FUNDS continued

Organization Name	Account Number	Number of Shares	Owner's Name(s) (exact name as on certificate)	Location

STOCKS

STOCKS

KNOW

You are halfway there. Keep up the good work.

BONDS

These include Treasury Notes (T-Bills), Zero Coupon Bond, War Bonds, and so on.

Type of Bond	Serial Number	Number of Shares	Owner's Name(s) (exact name as on certificate)	Location

BONDS continued

Type of Bond	Serial Number	Number of Shares	Owner's Name(s) (exact name as on certificate)	Location

STOCKS

ACTIONS/NOTES:

STOCKS

PROPERTY

PROPERTY

What do you own & can you prove you own it?

The majority of people own or lease vehicles, apartments, condominiums, or homes. It is recommended that you include copies or identify the location of ownership documents or contracts, such as deeds, registrations and leasing or rental agreements. Then when it is time for renewals, or if terms are being renegotiated or resolved, you have the necessary information well documented.

Additionally, consider including unique item numbers, such as vehicle identification numbers and license numbers. These are very important when property is lost or stolen and you need to report it to the authorities and insurance companies.

The last half of *Property* is where you keep a record of other significant property and personal items that you feel are important.

If you are using this book to support your tickler system, you can use this section to highlight the month when your property taxes are due, the month and year that you need to renew rental or leasing contracts, etc.

Completing *Property* prior to *Insurance* provides an excellent reference of checks and balances for reviewing what you need to cover in your insurance policies.

PROPERTY

KNOW YOUR LIFE - ORGANIZE YOUR PROPERTY!

KNOW

Protect yourself from identity theft. Protect this book.

VEHICLES (CAR, BOAT, MOTORCYCLE, JET SKI, etc.)

Type of Vehicle: _____

Manufacturer: _____ Model: _____ Year: _____

Color: _____ Vehicle Identification Number: _____

License Registration State: _____ Tag Number: _____

Ownership Document Number: _____

Location of Ownership Document: _____

Registrant's Name: _____

Type of Vehicle: _____

Manufacturer: _____ Model: _____ Year: _____

Color: _____ Vehicle Identification Number: _____

License Registration State: _____ Tag Number: _____

Ownership Document Number: _____

Location of Ownership Document: _____

Registrant's Name: _____

Type of Vehicle: _____

Manufacturer: _____ Model: _____ Year: _____

Color: _____ Vehicle Identification Number: _____

License Registration State: _____ Tag Number: _____

Ownership Document Number: _____

Location of Ownership Document: _____

Registrant's Name: _____

PROPERTY

KNOW

Enclosing copies of the actual ownership documents and/or contracts can be helpful down the road.

VEHICLES continued

Type of Vehicle: _____

Manufacturer: _____ Model: _____ Year: _____

Color: _____ Vehicle Identification Number: _____

License Registration State: _____ Tag Number: _____

Ownership Document Number: _____

Location of Ownership Document: _____

Registrant's Name: _____

Type of Vehicle: _____

Manufacturer: _____ Model: _____ Year: _____

Color: _____ Vehicle Identification Number: _____

License Registration State: _____ Tag Number: _____

Ownership Document Number: _____

Location of Ownership Document: _____

Registrant's Name: _____

Type of Vehicle: _____

Manufacturer: _____ Model: _____ Year: _____

Color: _____ Vehicle Identification Number: _____

License Registration State: _____ Tag Number: _____

Ownership Document Number: _____

Location of Ownership Document: _____

Registrant's Name: _____

REAL ESTATE

Includes houses, vacation homes, condominiums, rental properties, and so on.

Type: _____

Address: _____

_____

Location of Deed: _____ Location of Tax Bill: _____

Name of Owner(s): _____

Related Mortgage: _____

Type: _____

Address: _____

_____

Location of Deed: _____ Location of Tax Bill: _____

Name of Owner(s): _____

Related Mortgage: _____

Type: _____

Address: _____

_____

Location of Deed: _____ Location of Tax Bill: _____

Name of Owner(s): _____

Related Mortgage: _____

PROPERTY

REAL ESTATE continued

Type: _____

Address: _____

_____

Location of Deed: _____ Location of Tax Bill: _____

Name of Owner(s): _____

Related Mortgage: _____

Type: _____

Address: _____

_____

Location of Deed: _____ Location of Tax Bill: _____

Name of Owner(s): _____

Related Mortgage: _____

Type: _____

Address: _____

_____

Location of Deed: _____ Location of Tax Bill: _____

Name of Owner(s): _____

Related Mortgage: _____

LEASING DOCUMENTS

Includes apartments, homes, offices, storage, or timeshares that you rent from others.

Document: _____

Company Name: _____

Address: _____

_____

Location of Contract: _____

Signature(s) on Contract: _____

Renewal Date: _____

Document: _____

Company Name: _____

Address: _____

_____

Location of Contract: _____

Signature(s) on Contract: _____

Renewal Date: _____

PROPERTY

LEASING DOCUMENTS continued

Document: _____

Company Name: _____

Address: _____

_____

Location of Contract: _____

Signature(s) on Contract: _____

Renewal Date: _____

Document: _____

Company Name: _____

Address: _____

_____

Location of Contract: _____

Signature(s) on Contract: _____

Renewal Date: _____

Document: _____

Company Name: _____

Address: _____

_____

Location of Contract: _____

Signature(s) on Contract: _____

Renewal Date: _____

PROPERTY

KNOW

This book was developed to organize your life, not as a checklist of what you have to do in life.

ACTIONS/NOTES:

PROPERTY

INSURANCE

INSURANCE

INSURANCE

How are you protected?

It is important that you identify your various insurance policies and the physical location of the documents. Remember as with the other sections of this book, the potential types of insurance listed are not what you need to have, but a list of what you may have to document.

Additionally, you should record the valuables you have, their value and location, and a copy of any appraisals that you have on the items. Consider providing a visual record of the valuables with film or digital photos. If you provide photographs, include an object in the picture, such as a ruler or currency, to provide a reference for size. Also, because some items appreciate with time, consider including an object for date reference in the picture, such as a newspaper.

If you prefer, you can write who will inherit the object on the back of the photograph. If you opt to do this, mention that you are using this method in your legal will.

Finally, if you have had your valuables appraised, include the appraisal documents or copies of them in this section.

If you are using *Know Your Life* to support your tickler system, you can identify when insurance premiums are due or when you need to renew a policy for accurate coverage.

INSURANCE

KNOW YOUR LIFE - ORGANIZE YOUR INSURANCE!

KNOW

Talk to a professional about how to leave valuable items to family members.

INSURANCE

INSURANCE POLICIES

HOME

Company:_____

Policy Number:_____   Policy Location:_____

Agent's Name:_____   Agent's Phone:_____

Address:_____

_____

Location of Policy:_____

RENTERS

Company:_____

Policy Number:_____   Policy Location:_____

Agent's Name:_____   Agent's Phone:_____

Address:_____

_____

Location of Policy:_____

HOUSEHOLD GOODS

Company:_____

Policy Number:_____   Policy Location:_____

Agent's Name:_____   Agent's Phone:_____

Address:_____

_____

Location of Policy:_____

KNOW

Additional insurance coverage is often provided by employers, some associations, credit cards, frequent flyer programs, etc.

INSURANCE

INSURANCE POLICIES continued

VEHICLES

Company: _____

Policy Number: _____ Policy Location: _____

Agent's Name: _____ Agent's Phone: _____

Address: _____

_____

Location of Policy: _____

FLOOD

Company: _____

Policy Number: _____ Policy Location: _____

Agent's Name: _____ Agent's Phone: _____

Address: _____

_____

Location of Policy: _____

EARTHQUAKE

Company: _____

Policy Number: _____ Policy Location: _____

Agent's Name: _____ Agent's Phone: _____

Address: _____

_____

Location of Policy: _____

INSURANCE POLICIES continued

OTHER: _____

Company: _____

Policy Number: _____ Policy Location: _____

Agent's Name: _____ Agent's Phone: _____

Address: _____

_____

Location of Policy: _____

OTHER: _____

Company: _____

Policy Number: _____ Policy Location: _____

Agent's Name: _____ Agent's Phone: _____

Address: _____

_____

Location of Policy: _____

OTHER: _____

Company: _____

Policy Number: _____ Policy Location: _____

Agent's Name: _____ Agent's Phone: _____

Address: _____

_____

Location of Policy: _____

INSURANCE

LIFE INSURANCE POLICIES

Company: _____

Policy Number: _____   Policy Location: _____

Agent's Name: _____   Agent's Phone: _____

Address: _____

_____

Beneficiary: _____

Company: _____

Policy Number: _____   Policy Location: _____

Agent's Name: _____   Agent's Phone: _____

Address: _____

_____

Beneficiary: _____

Company: _____

Policy Number: _____   Policy Location: _____

Agent's Name: _____   Agent's Phone: _____

Address: _____

_____

Beneficiary: _____

INSURANCE

VALUABLES

Item/Description	Serial Number	Value	Location

INSURANCE

VALUABLES continued

Item/Description	Serial Number	Value	Location

INSURANCE

KNOW

Only two more chapters to go!

VALUABLES continued

Item/Description	Serial Number	Value	Location

VALUABLES continued

Item/Description	Serial Number	Value	Location

INSURANCE

VALUABLES continued

Item/Description	Serial Number	Value	Location

INSURANCE

INSURANCE

ACTIONS/NOTES:

INSURANCE

MEDICAL

MEDICAL

MEDICAL

Take care of yourself & those you care about.

The *Medical* section addresses any medical plans that you currently have and will depend on after you retire.

In this area include any personal and/or employer medical plans, Medicare, disability, long-term care, and supplemental insurance. The military provides some support to disabled and retired veterans, so veterans should document their military history in this section.

It is important to identify who the doctors are that provide you with healthcare and which hospitals you visit so that others know where to get your medical history information. The list of doctors should include: general practitioners, dentists, specialists, ophthalmologists, chiropractors, acupuncturists, etc.

Finally, if you have a living will this is a good section to identify the existence of such a document and its location. For further information on living wills, contact a lawyer, your local medical facility, or look at the library or on the Internet. Ensure that you give a current copy of your living will to your doctors to keep in your hospital records in the event that you are under their care with a major life-threatening problem.

MEDICAL

KNOW YOUR LIFE - ORGANIZE YOUR MEDICAL PLANS!

KNOW

If you have suggestions on how to improve this book, send them to suggestions@knowyourlife.com.

MEDICAL

LIVING WILL

(check one)

❏ No

❏ Yes - include a copy in this book or
       provide the locations of documents: _____

MEDICARE

Primary: _____ Number: _____ A / B

Partner: _____ Number: _____ A / B

Other: _____ Number: _____ A / B

Other: _____ Number: _____ A / B

MILITARY

It is recommended that you enclose a copy of the discharge papers and provide the location of the original copy. These papers will be necessary to identify if and what kind of medical support the government will provide the veteran.

Primary: _____

Partner: _____

MEDICAL POLICIES

Company/HMO: _____

Patient's Name: _____

Policy Number: _____ Policy Location: _____

Agent's Name: _____ Agent's Phone: _____

Address: _____

_____

Company/HMO: _____

Patient's Name: _____

Policy Number: _____ Policy Location: _____

Agent's Name: _____ Agent's Phone: _____

Address: _____

_____

Company/HMO: _____

Patient's Name: _____

Policy Number: _____ Policy Location: _____

Agent's Name: _____ Agent's Phone: _____

Address: _____

_____

MEDICAL

MEDICAL POLICIES continued

Company/HMO: _____

Patient's Name: _____

Policy Number: _____   Policy Location: _____

Agent's Name: _____   Agent's Phone: _____

Address: _____

_____

Company/HMO: _____

Patient's Name: _____

Policy Number: _____   Policy Location: _____

Agent's Name: _____   Agent's Phone: _____

Address: _____

_____

Company/HMO: _____

Patient's Name: _____

Policy Number: _____   Policy Location: _____

Agent's Name: _____   Agent's Phone: _____

Address: _____

_____

MEDICAL

KNOW

You can use sticky notes to mark the sections where and when monthly payments, renewals, or other actions are due.

MEDICAL

HOSPITALS

Hospital: _____

Specialty: _____

Patient's Name: _____

Doctor: _____

Assistant: _____

Address: _____ Phone: _____

_____

Do they have a copy of the living will? ❏ Yes ❏ No

Hospital: _____

Specialty: _____

Patient's Name: _____

Doctor: _____

Assistant: _____

Address: _____ Phone: _____

_____

Do they have a copy of the living will? ❏ Yes ❏ No

MEDICAL

HOSPITALS continued

Hospital: _____

Specialty: _____

Patient's Name: _____

Doctor: _____

Assistant: _____

Address: _____ Phone: _____

_____

Do they have a copy of the living will?   ❏ Yes   ❏ No

Hospital: _____

Specialty: _____

Patient's Name: _____

Doctor: _____

Assistant: _____

Address: _____ Phone: _____

_____

Do they have a copy of the living will?   ❏ Yes   ❏ No

MEDICAL

DOCTORS

Doctor: _____

Specialty: _____

Patient's Name: _____

Medical Assistant: _____

Address: _____   Phone: _____

_____

Do they have a copy of the living will?   ❑ Yes   ❑ No

Doctor: _____

Specialty: _____

Patient's Name: _____

Medical Assistant: _____

Address: _____   Phone: _____

_____

Do they have a copy of the living will?   ❑ Yes   ❑ No

Doctor: _____

Specialty: _____

Patient's Name: _____

Medical Assistant: _____

Address: _____   Phone: _____

_____

Do they have a copy of the living will?   ❑ Yes   ❑ No

MEDICAL

DOCTORS continued

Doctor: _____

Specialty: _____

Patient's Name: _____

Medical Assistant: _____

Address: _____ Phone: _____

_____

Do they have a copy of the living will?   ❏ Yes   ❏ No

Doctor: _____

Specialty: _____

Patient's Name: _____

Medical Assistant: _____

Address: _____ Phone: _____

_____

Do they have a copy of the living will?   ❏ Yes   ❏ No

Doctor: _____

Specialty: _____

Patient's Name: _____

Medical Assistant: _____

Address: _____ Phone: _____

_____

Do they have a copy of the living will?   ❏ Yes   ❏ No

MEDICAL

DOCTORS continued

Doctor: _____

Specialty: _____

Patient's Name: _____

Medical Assistant: _____

Address: _____ Phone: _____

_____

Do they have a copy of the living will?   ❑ Yes   ❑ No

Doctor: _____

Specialty: _____

Patient's Name: _____

Medical Assistant: _____

Address: _____ Phone: _____

_____

Do they have a copy of the living will?   ❑ Yes   ❑ No

Doctor: _____

Specialty: _____

Patient's Name: _____

Medical Assistant: _____

Address: _____ Phone: _____

_____

Do they have a copy of the living will?   ❑ Yes   ❑ No

MEDICAL

MEDICAL

ACTIONS/NOTES:

WISHES

WISHES

WISHES

What are your wishes for those around you?

This section provides guidance to those who will manage your affairs after you are no longer able to: whether you become disabled, or whether you die. In *Wishes*, you identify who has the authority to make decisions for you, including power of attorneys, wills, funeral arrangements, and contacts.

For some, this is the most difficult section to complete, as it speaks to the difficult as well as the inevitable. If you find this uncomfortable, it may make it easier to complete if you keep in mind that this book will help those experiencing the loss of a loved one.

Wishes is also a place to identify the various professionals and professional organizations that you work with in your life. Organizations are groups based on career specialties and/or market segments: universities, fraternities, sororities, military service groups, and/or community business groups such as the Chamber of Commerce, Roundtable, Toastmasters, etc.

Consider including a copy of any agreements that you have with professionals such as attorneys, mentors, politicians, professors, and so on. Be sure to attach their business card to either the page or the agreement.

The last item in *Wishes* is a list of the most precious belongings that you have and your instructions on what should happen to them when you are deceased. This list is in addition to the list of valuables that you identified in *Insurance*. These can be very personal items like wedding rings, earrings, a favorite gold chain, and heirlooms, like a family Bible, spoon or thimble collections, hats, tools, family pictures and films, Internet web domains, and who will maintain the family website.

Remember, if you are using the *Wishes* section as the way to identify who gets what, you need to notate that in your will and include the location where this book can be found.

For the survivors, it is helpful to use this book to hold copies of the death certificate. You will need several of these to give to financial institutions, insurance companies, retirement groups and so on, in order to validate that the individual has died.

KNOW YOUR LIFE - ORGANIZE YOUR WISHES!

KNOW

This book is invaluable to your loved ones.

WISHES

DOCUMENTS

The following are some common documents related to settling the estate of individuals. They are not necessary for everyone. I recommend that you talk to an advisor to determine which ones that you may need. Include a copy of these documents in this book for reference.

WILL

Location: _____

Point of Contact: _____

Address: _____ Phone: _____

_____

TRUST

Location: _____

Point of Contact: _____

Address: _____ Phone: _____

_____

NOTES

_____

_____

_____

_____

KNOW

Remind the executor of your Will about the existence and location of this book once a year.

WISHES

DURABLE POWER OF ATTORNEY

❏ Yes   ❏ No

Location: _____

Point of Contact: _____

Address: _____ Phone: _____

_____

FINANCIAL POWER OF ATTORNEY

❏ Yes   ❏ No

Location: _____

Point of Contact: _____

Address: _____ Phone: _____

_____

OTHER POWER OF ATTORNEY

Description: _____

Location: _____

Point of Contact: _____

Address: _____ Phone: _____

_____

WISHES

ATTORNEY

Attorney: _____

Specialty: _____

Law Firm: _____

Client: _____

Address: _____ Phone: _____

_____

Attorney: _____

Specialty: _____

Law Firm: _____

Client: _____

Address: _____ Phone: _____

_____

Attorney: _____

Specialty: _____

Law Firm: _____

Client: _____

Address: _____ Phone: _____

_____

FUNERAL

Preparation
Includes embalming, cremation, alternative casket, or body donation (identify the documents where donation is approved, such as driver's license or will):

_____

_____

_____

_____

Ceremony
Includes arrangements, wishes for viewing, celebration of life event, memorial, military funeral:

_____

_____

_____

_____

Burial
Includes plot location, deed, scattering location, urn, or coffin:

_____

_____

_____

_____

Funeral Home: _____

Address: _____ Phone: _____

_____

Location of any agreements or contracts: _____

KNOW

Check with your legal advisor in order to make your wishes legally binding.

RELIGIOUS ORGANIZATIONS

Name: _____

Point of Contact: _____

Address: _____ Phone: _____

_____

Name: _____

Point of Contact: _____

Address: _____ Phone: _____

_____

Name: _____

Point of Contact: _____

Address: _____ Phone: _____

_____

Name: _____

Point of Contact: _____

Address: _____ Phone: _____

_____

OBITUARY

Attach a write-up of what you desire in your obituary, or list key pieces of information (date and location of birth, father's and mother's name, names of children and grandchildren, accomplishments, awards, schools, degrees, military time and campaigns, associations, and organizations). Check your local paper for requirements and examples.

OBITUARY AND DEATH NOTICE PUBLICATIONS

List names of newspapers and publications that you want to have the obituary sent to.

Name of Publication: _____

Address: _____ Phone: _____

_____

Name of Publication: _____

Address: _____ Phone: _____

_____

Name of Publication: _____

Address: _____ Phone: _____

_____

Name of Publication: _____

Address: _____ Phone: _____

_____

WISHES

NOTIFICATION

List the people and organizations that you want to have notified of your passing. Provide name, relationship, phone numbers, and addresses including email if relevant, for each.

Name   Relationship   Phone   Address

_____

NOTIFICATION continued

Name	Relationship	Phone	Address

WISHES

NOTIFICATION continued

Name	Relationship	Phone	Address

NOTIFICATION continued

Name	Relationship	Phone	Address

WISHES

PROFESSIONAL ASSOCIATIONS

Association:_____ Chapter:_____

Member Name:_____ Membership Number:_____

Local Point of Contact:_____ Phone:_____

Headquarters Address:_____ Phone:_____

_____

Web Site Address:_____

Association:_____ Chapter:_____

Member Name:_____ Membership Number:_____

Local Point of Contact:_____ Phone:_____

Headquarters Address:_____ Phone:_____

_____

Web Site Address:_____

Association:_____ Chapter:_____

Member Name:_____ Membership Number:_____

Local Point of Contact:_____ Phone:_____

Headquarters Address:_____ Phone:_____

_____

Web Site Address:_____

WISHES

PROFESSIONAL ASSOCIATIONS continued

Association: _____ Chapter: _____

Member Name: _____ Membership Number: _____

Local Point of Contact: _____ Phone: _____

Headquarters Address: _____ Phone: _____

_____

Web Site Address: _____

Association: _____ Chapter: _____

Member Name: _____ Membership Number: _____

Local Point of Contact: _____ Phone: _____

Headquarters Address: _____ Phone: _____

_____

Web Site Address: _____

Association: _____ Chapter: _____

Member Name: _____ Membership Number: _____

Local Point of Contact: _____ Phone: _____

Headquarters Address: _____ Phone: _____

_____

Web Site Address: _____

WISHES

FRATERNAL/SOCIAL ORGANIZATIONS

Organization: _____ Chapter: _____

Member Name: _____ Membership Number: _____

Local Point of Contact: _____ Phone: _____

Headquarters Address: _____ Phone: _____

_____

Web Site Address: _____

Organization: _____ Chapter: _____

Member Name: _____ Membership Number: _____

Local Point of Contact: _____ Phone: _____

Headquarters Address: _____ Phone: _____

_____

Web Site Address: _____

Organization: _____ Chapter: _____

Member Name: _____ Membership Number: _____

Local Point of Contact: _____ Phone: _____

Headquarters Address: _____ Phone: _____

_____

Web Site Address: _____

WISHES

MOST PRECIOUS BELONGINGS

Item	Description/Serial Number	Location	Instructions

MOST PRECIOUS BELONGINGS continued

Item	Description/Serial Number	Location	Instructions

MOST PRECIOUS BELONGINGS continued

Item	Description/Serial Number	Location	Instructions

WISHES

MOST PRECIOUS BELONGINGS continued

Item	Description/Serial Number	Location	Instructions

KNOW

Congratulations!
You've organized your life.
For additional references
and suggestions, visit
www.knowyourlife.com

ACTIONS/NOTES:

ACTIONS/NOTES:

WISHES

ACTIONS/NOTES:

WISHES

INDEX

ABOUT THE AUTHOR

 Jim Litchko has managed various operational, budget, IT, business development, and strategic planning projects in commercial, military, government, and non-profit organizations. In the past thirty years he learned strategies to effectively organize routine and crisis tasks and prepare for unexpected events. He is a frequent keynoter, presenter, and facilitator as well as a professional member in the National Speakers Association. A student of Ken Blanchard, Ph.D., co-author of *The One Minute Manager*®, he holds a Masters degree in Information Systems from Johns Hopkins University and a Bachelors degree in Industrial Technology from Ohio University. Jim lives in Maryland with his wife of 32 years.

QUICK ORDER FORM

Give the gift of *Know Your Life* to your family, friends and colleagues
www.knowbookpublishing.com

❏ **YES!** Please send me _____ copies of *Know Your Life* for $19.95 USD, $28.95 Canadian each.

❏ **YES!** I am interested in having James P. Litchko speak or give a seminar at my company, association, school or organization. Please send me more information.

Shipping: Within the U.S. include $3.95 USD shipping & handling for one book, and $3.00 for each additional book. Canadian orders include $5.95 Canadian for one book and $4.00 Canadian for each additional book.

Sales tax: Maryland residents add 5% sales tax on each book.

Payment must accompany orders. Allow 3 weeks for delivery.

My payment of $ _____ is enclosed.
Make check or money order payable to **Know Book Publishing**.

Please charge my: ❏ VISA   ❏ MASTERCARD   ❏ AMERICAN EXPRESS

Name: _____

Organization: _____

Address: _____

City/State/Zip: _____

Phone: _____   E-mail: _____

Name on Card: _____   Card Number: _____

Exp. Date: _____   Signature: _____

Fax orders: 240-363-0231. Send this completed form. Credit card orders only.

Web orders: Visit http://knowyourlife.com to order via the Internet.

Postal orders: Mail to: Know Your Life
　　　　　　　　　　　Book Order Department
　　　　　　　　　　　P.O. Box G
　　　　　　　　　　　Kensington, MD. 20895